CAMERAS

© Aladdin Books Ltd 1990

*First published in
the United States in 1991 by*
Gloucester Press
387 Park Avenue South
New York, NY 10016

Design David West
Children's Book Design

Editor Roger Vlitos

Editorial Planning Lionheart Books

Researcher Emma Krikler

Illustrator Alex Pang and Ian Moores

Printed in Belgium

Library of Congress Cataloging-in-Publication Data

Graham, Ian. 1953-
　　　Cameras / Ian Graham.
　　　　p. cm.　--　(How it works)
　　　Includes index.
　　　Summary: Explains how a camera functions,
describes all its working parts, traces its
development and advances, and instructs in how to
achieve special effects when using a camera.
　　　ISBN 0-531-17280-5
　　　1. Cameras--Juvenile literature. [1. Cameras.] I.
Title. II. Series: How it works (Gloucester Press)
TR149.G73　　　1991
771.3--dc20　　　　　　　90-43982　CIP　　AC

CONTENTS

HOW · IT · WORKS
CAMERAS

IAN GRAHAM

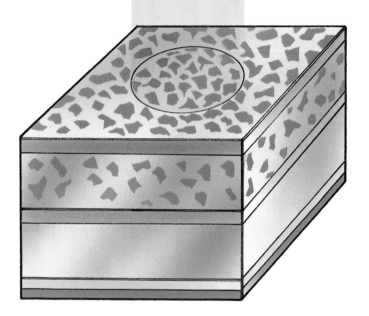

GLOUCESTER PRESS

New York · London · Toronto · Sydney

THE WORKING PARTS

A camera is a device designed specially to record images on light-sensitive film. There are many different types of camera, but they all work in much the same way. The Single-Lens Reflex, or SLR, camera shown here is an example of one of the most popular types.

A camera is basically a lightproof box. A lens is fixed to one side and film is positioned inside the box opposite the lens. Light is prevented from entering the box by a shutter, a type of blind, behind the lens. When closed, the shutter stops light passing through a hole, the aperture, in the camera body. Light entering the lens of an SLR is reflected upward by a mirror. At the top of this camera, a specially shaped block of glass called a penta-prism reflects the light out through the viewfinder. Other types of cameras have separate view-finder and shutter-lens systems.

When a camera user wishes to take a photograph, or "shot," almost the exact image that will be recorded on the film can be seen in the viewfinder. At the right moment, the shutter is opened by pressing a button known as the shutter release. If the camera is an SLR, the mirror flips up out of the way, allowing the light to pass through the lens and reach the film. The lens bends the rays of light so that they produce a sharp image on the film. The amount the light rays have to be bent, or refracted, depends on how far away the objects are from the camera. Refraction is adjusted by rotating the focusing ring on the lens. Some cameras use a fixed-focus lens that is suitable for photo-

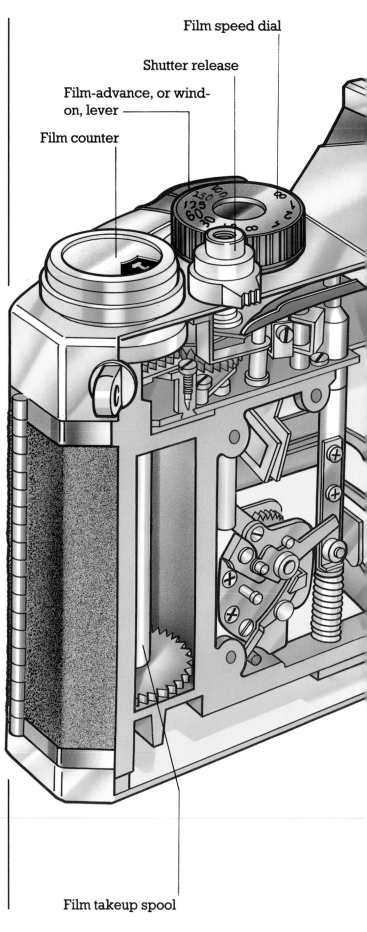

Film speed dial

Shutter release

Film-advance, or wind-on, lever

Film counter

Film takeup spool

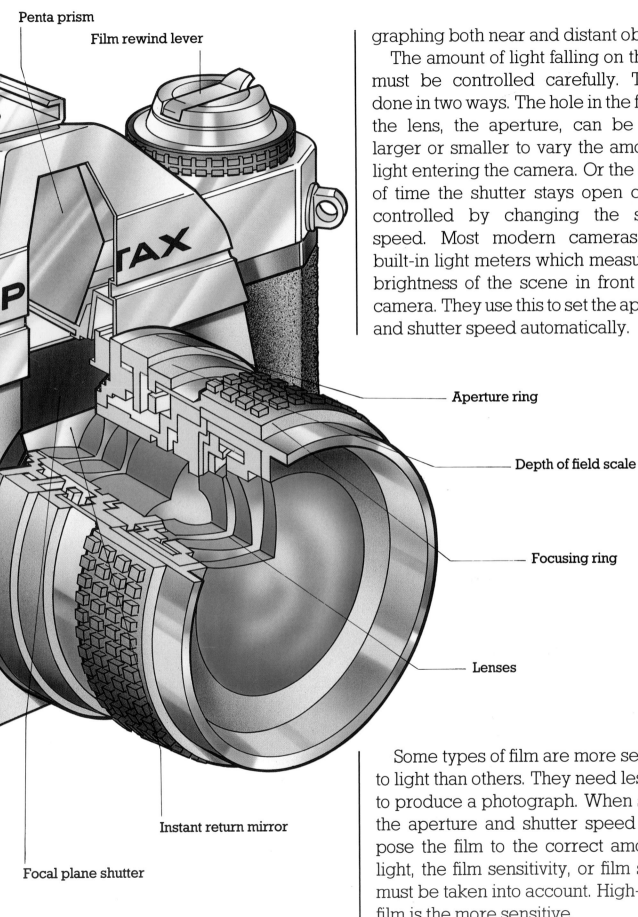

Penta prism

Film rewind lever

P TAX

Aperture ring

Depth of field scale

Focusing ring

Lenses

Instant return mirror

Focal plane shutter

graphing both near and distant objects.

The amount of light falling on the film must be controlled carefully. This is done in two ways. The hole in the front of the lens, the aperture, can be made larger or smaller to vary the amount of light entering the camera. Or the length of time the shutter stays open can be controlled by changing the shutter speed. Most modern cameras have built-in light meters which measure the brightness of the scene in front of the camera. They use this to set the aperture and shutter speed automatically.

Some types of film are more sensitive to light than others. They need less light to produce a photograph. When setting the aperture and shutter speed to expose the film to the correct amount of light, the film sensitivity, or film speed, must be taken into account. High-speed film is the more sensitive.

5

DIFFERENT TYPES

Some cameras are small, inexpensive to buy and easy to use. Others are large, heavy and relatively complicated. Each different type of camera has been designed with a particular type of work and camera-user in mind.

Small pocket cameras use narrow film only 16mm across known as 110 size. Subminiature cameras use even smaller film. The most popular film size, or format, is 35mm, which uses 35mm-wide film. Most cameras use roll-film, with 12, 24 or 36 shots, or exposures, per roll, but some use large sheets of film.

There are two main types of 35mm camera – direct-vision and reflex. Direct-vision types are fitted with a simple peephole sight to enable the photographer to point the camera in the right direction. This type of viewfinder is separate from the lens that focuses the image on the film. The disadvantage here is that the photographer does not see exactly the same view that will form the image on the film.

Reflex cameras use a viewfinder system with a mirror to reflect light. A twin-lens reflex camera has two identical lenses. One focuses the image on the film, the other forms the same image in the viewfinder. The single-lens reflex camera is more popular. The lens that will focus the image on the film also forms the viewfinder image.

The 35mm single-lens reflex (opposite left) is popular with advanced amateur and professional photographers. The disc camera is unique in using a flat disc of film, giving the camera its slim shape. The twin-lens reflex camera (top left) is simpler than the SLR and has a viewfinder system in which you can see the object you wish to photograph while the film is being exposed. Cameras designed to use film pre-loaded into cartridges (middle left) make film loading easier and quicker. The largest cameras (left), designed for use in professional studios, are modern versions of 19th century plate cameras. A sheet of film is inserted and exposed only when focusing is complete. Amateur movie cameras (above) usually take 18 still photographs every second. When the film is run through a projector at the same speed, it gives the impression of realistic movement.

LENSES AND FOCUSING

The basic job of a camera lens is to form a sharp image on the film. Without a lens, the picture would be blurred. The simplest camera lens is a single piece of glass or plastic, shaped like a magnifying glass. More advanced cameras use sophisticated lenses called compound lenses. These are made by combining closely several different simple lenses, or elements. Compound lenses produce clearer and brighter pictures because they allow more light to reach the film and they correct faults in the simple lens, particularly those that distort the colors or blur the edges.

The image is focused by rotating the lens's focusing ring. In the viewfinder of an SLR camera, the photographer sees the image become less and less blurred until it is sharply focused. Some cameras have interchangeable lenses. One lens can be taken off the camera and easily replaced by a different lens that makes objects appear larger or smaller.

A camera is usually supplied with a standard lens already fitted. Mostly, this has a focal length of about 50mm. This means that it will bend inward rays of light from a distant object so that they all meet 50mm from the center of the lens. Lenses that make objects appear smaller, but get in more of a scene, have shorter focal lengths. They are called wide-angle lenses. More "powerful" lenses with longer focal lengths make objects appear larger in the photograph. They are called telephoto lenses. A zoom lens allows the focal length to be varied from, say, 100mm to 200mm. It offers the photographer a greater range of photo compositions.

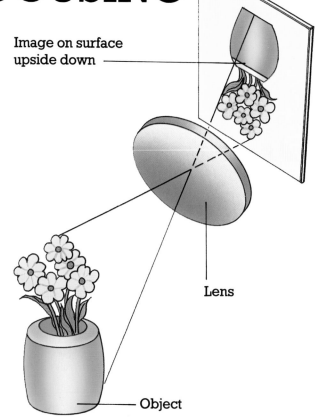

Image on surface upside down

Lens

Object

A single lens, also called a simple lens, will focus rays from an object to form an image on a screen. Because the light rays from the top and bottom of the object cross over at the lens, the image is upside down and reversed left to right compared to the object.

Wide-angle lens

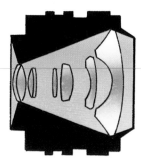

The view through a fish-eye lens. With its wide angle of view, a circular image is formed.

Standard lens

Telephoto lens

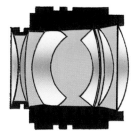

A fast shutter speed can "freeze" actions that would otherwise appear as a blur.

The diaphragm shutter, also called a leaf shutter, is a ring of metal segments, or leaves. When the shutter release is pressed, the segments rotate and move apart, opening up a hole, or aperture, through which light can pass to the film. While the diaphragm shutter opens up to expose the whole film, the focal plane shutter exposes a vertical window which passes across the film. The shutter is composed from two blinds, or blades. When the shutter release is pressed, the first blind snaps back, exposing the film. Then the second blind snaps across, covering the film again. The time separating the two blind movements is set by the shutter speed. This may be 1/2,000 of a second. The shorter the time, the narrower the gap between the two blinds. For speeds slower than 1/60 of a second, the first blind exposes all the frame.

The leaf shutter

A: Closed

Focal plane shutter

A: 1st blind moves

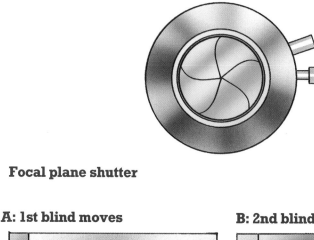

B: 2nd blind follo

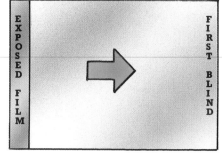

THE SHUTTER

A camera's shutter controls the length of time that light is allowed to fall on the film. Many cameras allow the photographer to choose a shutter speed ranging from as little as 1/2,000th of a second up to several seconds. Each speed is half of the one before. The range might be, say, 1/2,000th, 1/1,000th, 1/500th and so on. There may also be a 'B' setting that lets the photographer open and close the shutter manually to obtain exposures of several minutes or even hours. The shutter speed is selected either automatically by the camera's electronics or manually by rotating the shutter speed dial.

The shutter may be one of two types – the diaphragm shutter or the focal plane shutter. Most compact cameras are fitted with the diaphragm type of shutter. It is usually positioned within the lens, between the lens elements. If more advanced cameras fitted with interchangeable lenses used diaphragm shutters, each lens would have to have its own shutter mechanism, making the lenses very expensive. It makes more sense to build the shutter into the camera body. This is the focal plane shutter, so-called because it is placed just in front of the plane (a flat surface) where the image is focused on the film.

The diaphragm shutter opens to expose the whole film evenly at once. At shutter speeds shorter than about 1/30th of a second, the focal plane shutter opens to form a type of window which sweeps across the film.

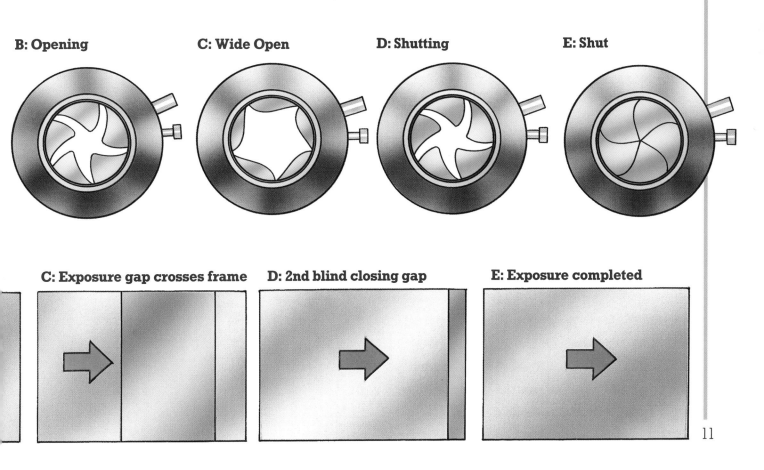

B: Opening **C: Wide Open** **D: Shutting** **E: Shut**

C: Exposure gap crosses frame **D: 2nd blind closing gap** **E: Exposure completed**

11

THE DIAPHRAGM

A camera's diaphragm works in the same way as the iris functions in the human eye. In bright sunshine, the iris closes down to reduce the amount of light entering the eye. In a darkened room, it opens up to let in more light.

A camera's diaphragm must therefore be opened up or closed down to control the amount of light entering the camera and falling on the film. It is necessary to control the amount of light in this way because exposing the film to too much light (known as overexposure) or too little light (underexposure) will spoil the photograph.

The diaphragm consists of a ring of overlapping metal blades. When the aperture ring around the outside of the lens is rotated by the photographer, the diaphragm blades swing around and a hole, or aperture, opens in the middle. The more the ring is turned, the bigger the aperture grows.

A lens's aperture is indicated by its f-number or f-stop. The f-number is calculated by dividing the lens's focal length by the diameter of its aperture. A 50mm lens with a 25mm aperture is therefore set to f2. Similar lenses set to the same f-stop will allow about the same amount of light through.

A camera's aperture ring usually has a number of click-stops so that it can be set to a series of known apertures. The click-stops are chosen so that each allows twice the amount of light through compared to the previous one. The higher the f-number, the smaller the aperture. So f11 is half the brightness of f8 and twice that of f16.

Print from underexposed negative film.

Print from overexposed negative film.

f2.8   f4

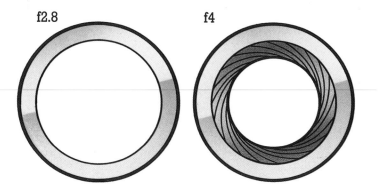

Depth of field

When a camera lens is focused on something, some objects closer to the camera and some that are further away are in focus too. The distance between the closest and furthest objects in focus is referred to as the depth of field.

Smaller apertures produce a greater depth of field than larger apertures. Short focal length lenses have a greater depth of field than long focal length lenses. Depth of field can be used, for example, to make an object stand out from blurred surroundings by choosing a wide aperture with a small depth of field.

At f16, all three objects are in focus.

At f2, only the middle object is in focus.

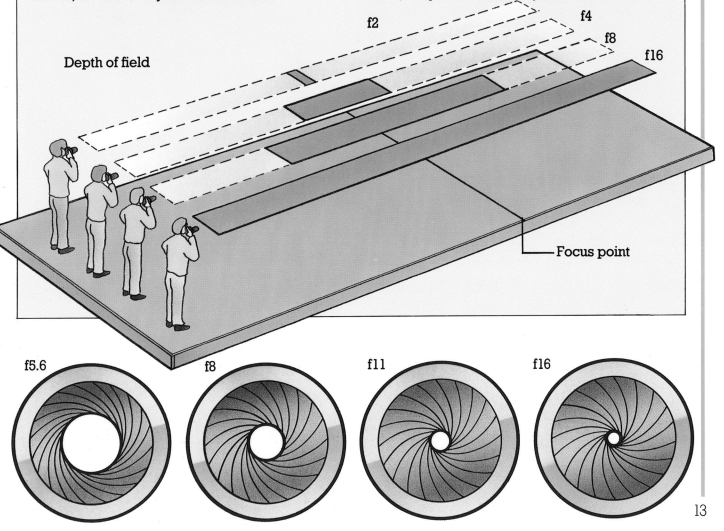

Depth of field

f2   f4   f8   f16

Focus point

f5.6   f8   f11   f16

BLACK AND WHITE FILM

Black and white film is made from a strip of plastic coated with a layer of silver compounds called silver halides. The strip is rolled up into a tiny can or cassette and loaded into the camera. Each time the camera's shutter release is pressed, a piece of film, or frame, is exposed to light.

In places where bright light strikes the film, the silver halides change to grains of silver. Other parts of the film remain unchanged. The exposed film is moved along by pulling a lever on top of the camera so that a fresh piece of film is ready for the next photograph.

Developing the exposed roll of film

Black and white film

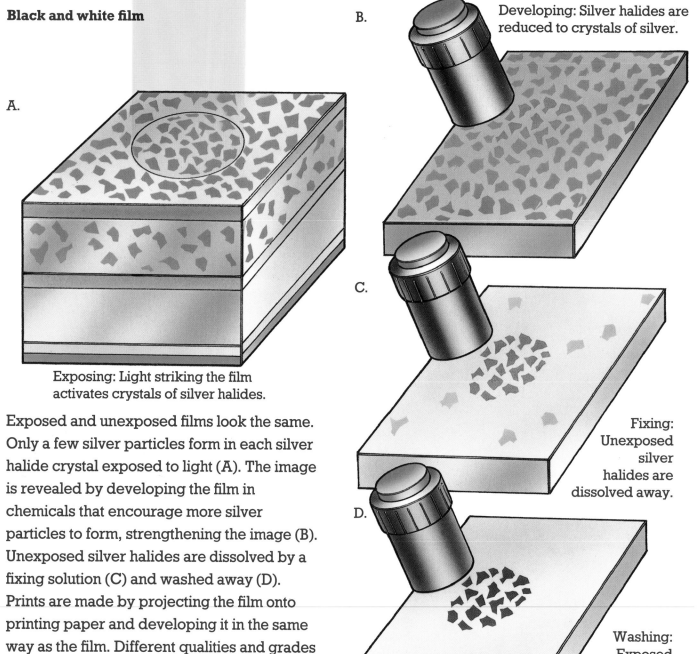

A.

Exposing: Light striking the film activates crystals of silver halides.

B.

Developing: Silver halides are reduced to crystals of silver.

C.

Fixing: Unexposed silver halides are dissolved away.

D.

Washing: Exposed areas remain as black deposits of silver.

Exposed and unexposed films look the same. Only a few silver particles form in each silver halide crystal exposed to light (A). The image is revealed by developing the film in chemicals that encourage more silver particles to form, strengthening the image (B). Unexposed silver halides are dissolved by a fixing solution (C) and washed away (D). Prints are made by projecting the film onto printing paper and developing it in the same way as the film. Different qualities and grades of paper produce photographs in which the tiny particles are apparent to varying amounts.

14

involves dissolving and washing away the unexposed silver halides, leaving a copy of the original scene. This is called a negative because the brightest parts of the scene are the blackest on the film.

To obtain a positive image that looks like the original scene, a "print" of the negative is made on special light-sensitive photographic paper. The negative is placed in a machine called an enlarger. This projects the negative image onto the printing paper. When the paper has been exposed, it is developed in the same way as the film.

In this close-up of a black and white print, particles of silver metal show up as black dots.

COLOR FILMS

Color film has a more complicated structure than black and white film. It resembles three black and white films sandwiched together. Each layer is made sensitive to a different main, or primary, color. For films, there are three primary colors – red, green and blue. (For paints, the primary colors are red, blue and yellow.) If all three are mixed together equally, they combine to produce white light. By varying the amounts of these three colors in the mixture, any color in the rainbow can be made. By making the three layers, or emulsions, of a color film sensitive to the three primary colors, the film can record images in full color.

There are two types of color film. One produces a negative when it is developed and this is used to make prints. The second type, called reversal film, produces color slides or transparencies, when developed.

Most color films are manufactured so that they produce realistic colors in natural daylight conditions. Some are specially produced for photographing in artificial light, as in a studio.

Each layer of color film reacts to a different color (A). The top layer records blue, the middle green and the bottom red. Other colors are recorded in more than one layer. White light activates all three as it is made up of all the colors of the rainbow.

The film is developed in a similar way to black and white film in order to change exposed silver halides to silver (B). Colored dyes are activated where silver forms. The negative image is revealed when the silver is dissolved away chemically (C).

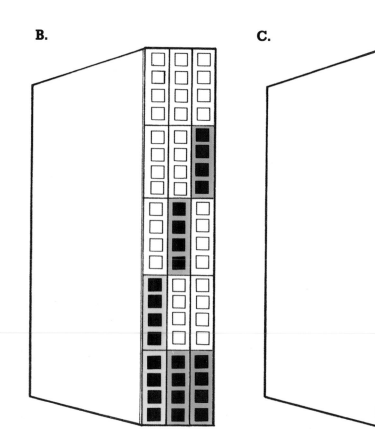

A.   B.   C.

Instant pictures

Light passes through the lens of this instant picture camera and bounces off a mirror onto the film. Each exposed frame of film is automatically pushed out of the camera between a pair of rollers which squeeze together the film, chemical developer and fixer. The image then forms in daylight after about a minute.

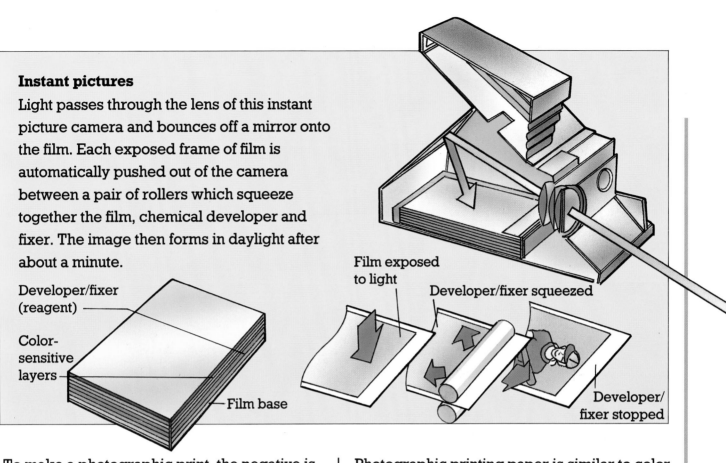

Developer/fixer (reagent)

Color-sensitive layers

Film base

Film exposed to light

Developer/fixer squeezed

Developer/fixer stopped

To make a photographic print, the negative is loaded into an enlarger and projected onto a sheet of photographic paper (D). The f-stop and exposure time for the paper are adjusted to the brightness of the negative – a dark negative needs longer exposure.

Photographic printing paper is similar to color film and it is developed in a similar way (E). During development, the unnatural negative colors are transformed chemically into the original lifelike colors so as to reproduce the scene (F).

D.

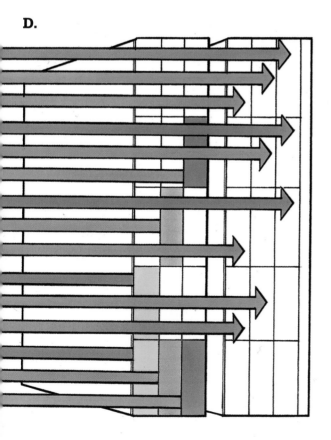

E.

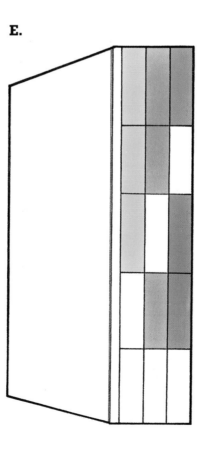

F.

TAKING A PHOTO

Taking a photograph is a curious mixture of science and art. The science is in operating the camera and its systems correctly. The art is in deciding what parts of a scene should be included in the photograph, where objects should be in relation to one another, the length of the exposure, and choosing the right moment to take the photograph.

Every time a camera's shutter release button is pressed a photograph may be taken. But merely pointing a camera at something of interest and pressing the shutter release would probably give rather disappointing results.

The photographer has to think about where to take the photograph from. A low viewpoint might give better or more interesting results than a high viewpoint. A close-up might be better than a long shot taken from further away.

If the camera has interchangeable lenses, the choice of lens is important too. The image should fill the viewfinder. It might be necessary to use a more powerful telephoto lens to magnify the image sufficiently.

The choice of shutter speed and f-stop is important. If a slow shutter speed is used to photograph a fast-moving object like a running horse, the horse may appear blurred in the picture because it was moving while the shutter was open but a fast shutter speed will "freeze" the action. With slow shutter speeds, camera shake is more likely.

The photographer loads the camera with a fresh roll of film and sets the film speed dial (1) to the speed printed on the film cassette, usually given as an ASA or ISO number.

The shutter speed (2) and lens aperture (3) are set. The camera may do these automatically or the photographer may set them manually.

It is important to hold a camera steady to avoid shaking it and blurring the photograph.

The photographer aims the camera at the scene to be photographed and focuses the lens (4) until the image in the viewfinder is clear and sharp.

The shutter release button is slowly pressed to take the photograph (5). The film wind-on lever is operated (6) to move a fresh piece of film into place for the next photograph.

FLASH AND LIGHTING

The word photography comes from two Greek words, phos and graphos, meaning light and drawing. Photography is drawing with light. Most photographs are taken in natural sunlight. But there are times when daylight does not give satisfactory results. The sky may be overcast. Even on a bright day, the subject may be in deep shadow or the film may not be light-sensitive enough for the conditions.

The answer is to provide artificial light. In the studio, professional photographers use a range of flood and flash lights, spotlights and reflectors to create the desired effect. Outside, photographers use electronic flashguns as a compact and lightweight source of light. The flashgun is connected to the camera so that a flash of light occurs when the shutter is fully open. This is called synchronized flash. As a focal plane shutter exposes only part of the film frame at a time when using fast shutter speeds, cameras with this system are usually synchronized with flash at a setting of 1/60th of a second or below.

▶ An electronic flashgun converts the low voltage from a battery pack into a very high voltage. When the camera's shutter opens, the high voltage is switched to a gas-filled flash tube. The surge of electricity causes tiny particles in the gas to be boosted with energy. They race to either of two metal plates (electrodes). Collisions between the particles result in some of their energy being released in a burst of intense light.

A scene is captured on film with flash.

Flash tube

Flashgun

Electrode

Electrons (atomic particles)

Mercury vapor (gas)

Electrode

The studio shot

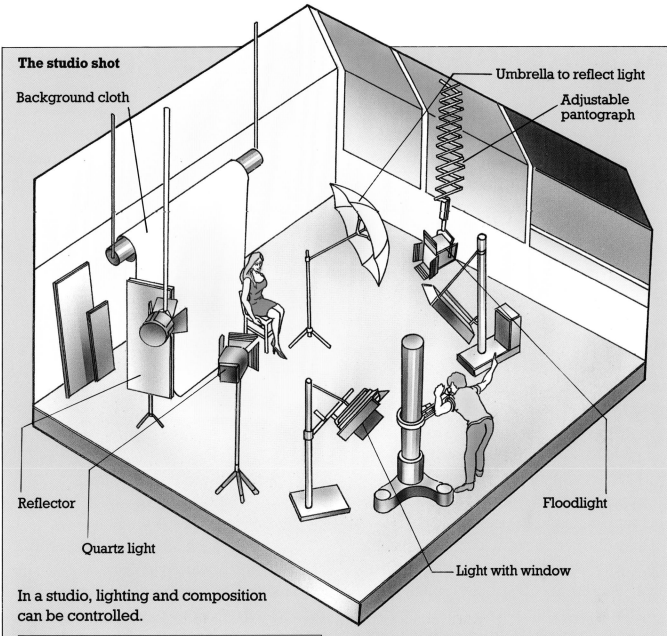

Background cloth

Umbrella to reflect light

Adjustable pantograph

Reflector

Quartz light

Floodlight

Light with window

In a studio, lighting and composition can be controlled.

Studio Lights

Within a studio, a photographer will use a range of light reflectors and lamps to create the desired lighting. Large reflectors used with "diffused" glass bulbs give soft, general illumination. Reflectors with polished surfaces used with small, clear glass lamps give hard lighting with sharp-edged shadows. Spotlights are fitted with various hoods and blinkers to concentrate their light onto a small area. Lights are supported on stands or suspended from the ceiling. The direction and strength of each light's illumination can be adjusted as required.

ACCESSORIES AND EFFECTS

Photographers frequently use a range of accessories either to help them take a photograph or to change the look or appearance of the photograph. Photos can be blurred by camera shake. To eliminate this, the camera can be mounted on a steady support such as a tripod. The camera may still shake when the shutter release is pressed. A cable release allows the shutter to be operated without touching the camera.

If the photographer is a long way from the camera, the shutter release may be operated by a sound switch that reacts to loud noises, or an infrared (heat-sensitive) remote control. A tripod can be cumbersome if the photographer has to move around. A one-legged mono-pod may be used in preference.

Lens filters are used to create special color effects or to eliminate color problems. A range of special lenses and screens are available to create effects including starbursts from bright points of light and multiple images.

Some photographers use a hand-held light meter. One popular type of light meter uses a light-sensitive cell. The amount of electrical current flowing from a battery changes depending on the amount of light falling on the cell. The brighter the light, the stronger the current. The current is measured and shown as an amount of light by a needle on a scale. This value is transferred to a calculator in the meter. When the calculator is set with film speed and light value, a range of suitable apertures and shutter speeds is displayed. The chosen settings are dialled into the camera.

The effect of a graduated color filter.

Color filters can make an ordinary photograph look extraordinary. Graduated color filters can, with color films, make a pale sky bluer or dried-up lawns appear green. A polarizing filter can be used to remove reflections from water. With black and white films, they increase contrast.

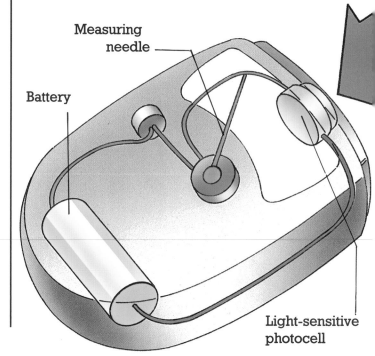

Measuring needle

Battery

Light-sensitive photocell

Livening up a photo by using a starburst filter.

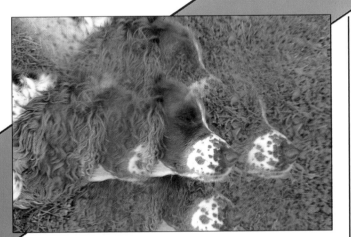
Multiple images created by a prism lens.

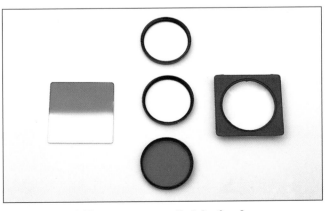
A range of filters are available for lenses.

Accessories

Tripods and monopods are available in a wide range of sizes, from tiny tabletop supports to massive stands used for studio work. The most commonly used type of camera support is the lightweight portable tripod with three telescopic legs and a central column that can be raised or lowered. A pan-and-tilt platform fitted to the top of the column enables the photographer to point the camera accurately, or follow movement steadily, without having to move the tripod itself.

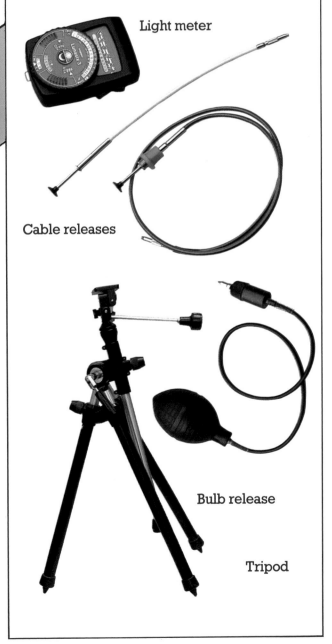
Light meter

Cable releases

Bulb release

Tripod

MOVING PICTURES

Movie cameras are very similar to "still" cameras. Both take static photographs. The difference is that a still camera takes just one photograph each time the shutter release is pressed, but a movie camera takes 18 to 24 still pictures every second. Amateur movies are usually made at 18 frames per second (fps) and professional movies at 24 fps. When the film is projected onto a screen at this speed, the rapidly changing images give the impression of movement. Amateur movies are made with reversal film, the same as slide film in still photography. Professional moviemakers use negative film. The "prints" shown in the theater are taken from these negatives. There is a range of different movie film sizes. *Super 8* is the most popular home movie format. Each frame is 8mm wide. Theater movies are made with 35mm or 70mm film.

The home movie camera (top right) has declined in popularity in favor of home video systems. Video offers two advantages: instant replay of recordings without having to wait for film to be developed, and a recording medium, magnetic tape, that can be used over and over again.

By taking one photograph at a time of a drawing or model, which is changed or moved between exposures, animated films can be made (middle right).

Theater movies are shown on much bigger screens than home movies. To ensure that such large images are sharp, theater movies can be made with larger film formats (right). The films are usually projected at the same frame-speed they were taken.

The movie camera

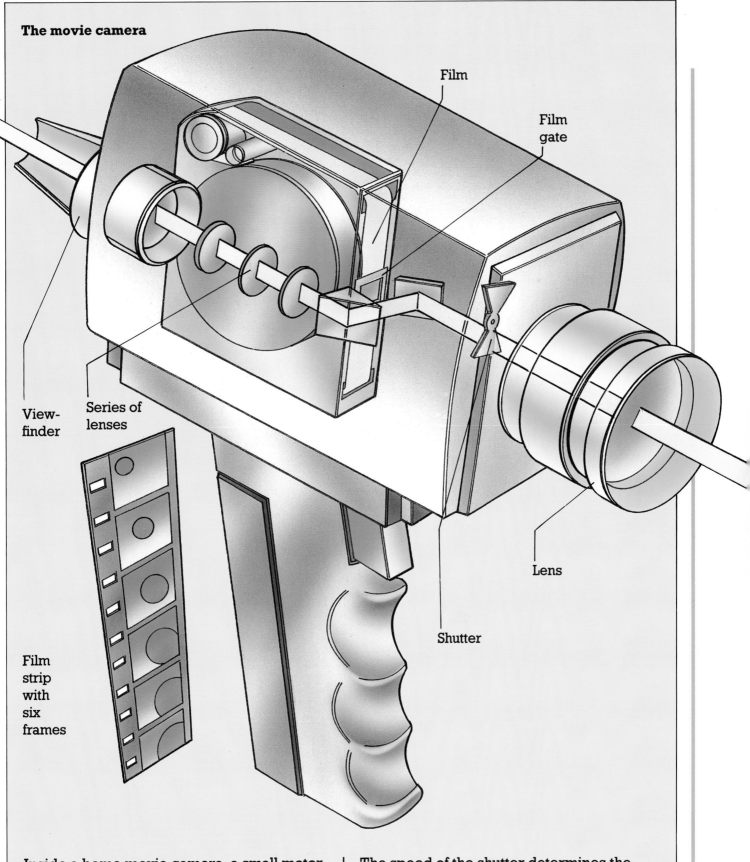

Film

Film gate

View-finder

Series of lenses

Lens

Shutter

Film strip with six frames

Inside a home movie camera, a small motor feeds film from a spool or a cassette past an aperture called the film gate. A propeller-like shutter revolves in front of the gate.

The speed of the shutter determines the number of still pictures, or frames, that are taken every second. A similar system exists in the projector.

SPECIAL CAMERAS

Some cameras are very specialized. They may be designed to do only one particular type of photographic work. They do exactly the same thing as the family snapshot camera in that they capture images on film, but at least one aspect of the camera is highly developed. Some have very advanced lenses to process the image in a unique way, as in the panoramic camera. Another type may be attached to additional instruments to obtain images from inaccessible places.

In medicine, cameras are often used to record images from inside the human body. X ray cameras use large sheets of film sensitive to both visible light and X rays. Instant picture cameras are used to take photos from ultrasound equipment (scanners) used to monitor the progress of unborn babies. The TV-type screens of computers and views through microscopes are often photographed to record experimental results.

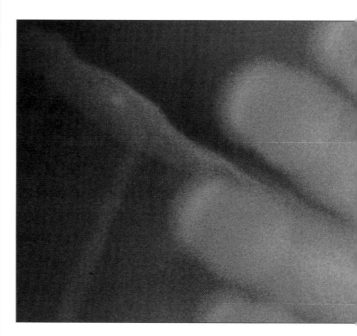

By using rotating mirrors or lenses, panoramic cameras can record up to a full circle of view, or a long row, in a single photograph (top). The view through a medical instrument such as an endoscope (middle), used to look inside the body, can be photographed by attaching a camera to it. Cameras on board aircraft photograph the ground in order to prepare maps or even to spy on enemy airfields and harbors. Those on diving equipment can photograph underwater life (right). Stereo cameras (far right) take two photographs from slightly different views. When the photos are looked at together in a special viewer, a three-dimensional effect is created.

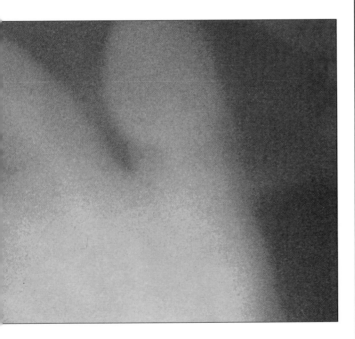

Holograms

All photographs taken with conventional cameras show scenes where everything appears flat. A special type of photograph called a hologram, made using the intense beam of light from a laser, shows three-dimensional scenes. You can look around objects in the foreground and see what is behind them. Holograms can be produced only with highly specialized and expensive equipment. They cannot be taken with ordinary cameras.

An illusion created by a hologram.

THE HISTORY OF CAMERAS

The word camera comes from the Latin "camera obscura" which means "darkened room." For hundreds of years people knew that an image of a bright scene could be projected through a tiny aperture onto a wall in a darkened room. However, it was not until 1827 that Joseph Niepce claimed to be able to "fix the images from a camera obscura." Using an asphalt varnish as his light-sensitive material he captured the view through his window – but the picture needed an eight hour exposure!

A camera obscura has an upside down and reversed image, as in a pinhole camera.

In 1837 Parisian Louis Daguerre, produced "daguerreotypes." These one-off positives needed 15-30 minutes of exposure. In England, William Henry Fox Talbot made tiny negatives, after half-hour exposures, in cameras which his wife called "mousetraps." New lenses, by the Hungarian Josef Petzval, improved exposure times greatly. Soon Fox Talbot made negatives in less than a minute, and then multiple prints from each which he called calotypes.

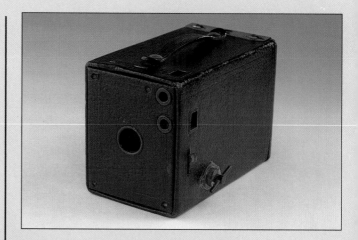

The popular Kodak box camera.

These inventions became obsolete when a process called wet-plate collodian came out in 1851, but a photographer still needed to be something of a chemist to take a successful picture. In 1888 American George Eastman introduced the light and portable kodax box camera which took 100 exposures on a roll of film, but the camera itself had to be sent back to the factory to process the film. By 1900 the Kodak "Brownie" was on sale to the general public at a cheap price, and films could be loaded separately. Popular photography was born.

An early Leica camera.

The first precision 35mm camera, the Leica, was made in Germany in 1925. It paved the way for a revolution in photography. The development of tiny electronic circuits led to cameras with built-in light meters and exposure control systems. In recent years the demand for simple "point-and-shoot" cameras produced the fully automatic 35mm compact, the smaller 110 pocket, and the slim, easy to load, disc cameras. The development of miniature electronic motors has allowed for built-in film winders.

A Nikon SLR, an electronic camera.

Video and computer-based imaging are beginning to rival film. By the end of the 1990s, movie studios will have begun to change over from film to high-definition video. Computers can store pictures in the form of a stream of numbers on a magnetic disc. Filmless cameras like the Sony Mavica work in this way. Developments in computerized imaging systems are advancing rapidly, as the enormous computing power needed to process high-quality images continues to become less costly.

FACTS AND FIGURES

The first negative photo was taken in 1835 by William Henry Fox Talbot, 18 years after Niepce captured the first photographic image.

The films used now are so sensitive that they can capture images in exposures that are 20 million times shorter than those used by the earliest photographers like Daguerre and Fox Talbot.

The first photograph taken from the air was taken from a balloon over Paris in 1858 by Gaspard Félix Tournachon.

A 35mm color negative contains the equivalent, in computer terms, of 72 million bits of information.

The fastest camera in the world is an electronic camera used for laser research at London's Imperial College. It can record images at the rate of 33,000 million every second.

The largest theater screens in the world are found in IMAX cinemas. The screens can be 18 meters high and 25 meters across. To obtain sharp images this size, IMAX cameras use a huge film format. The frame is ten times the size of a 35mm frame used in normal camera films.

The earliest process for adding sound to a movie was developed by Eugene Augustin Lauste in 1906. He produced a working system in London in 1910.

GLOSSARY

Accessory shoe
A fitting on top of a camera. Accessories such as a flashgun can be plugged into it. The shoe has electrical contacts to link a flashgun to the camera electronics.

Aperture
The hole in the front of a camera or lens that light passes through to reach the film. The size of the aperture is adjustable on most cameras.

ASA
An American standard measure of film speed, replaced by **ISO**.

Depth of field
The distance between the closest point and the furthest point of an image that are in sharp focus.

Diaphragm shutter
A camera shutter made from overlapping metal leaves which swivel open to expose the film when the shutter release button is pressed.

DIN
Deutsche Industrie Norm, the German standards organization and, in photography, the film speed system based on their standards. Now replaced by **ISO**.

Emulsion
A layer or layers of silver salt (iodide, chloride or bromide) crystals in gelatin used to coat a range of plastics, glass and papers to make light-sensitive materials for photography, including 35mm roll film.

Enlarger
A device used to project images on negatives onto light-sensitive paper to make positive prints or photographs.

Filmless camera
A camera that uses a medium other than film for recording images, such as magnetic tape.

Filter
A colored glass or plastic sheet used to change a photograph's appearance.

Focal plane shutter
A type of camera shutter made from two sliding blinds. One snaps back to expose the film and the second snaps across to cover it up again.

ISO
International Standardization Organization. In photography, a speed rating for film that has replaced **ASA** and **DIN**.

Latent image
The invisible image on an exposed film that is revealed by developing the film.

Panning
A way of photographing moving objects by moving the camera in the same direction as the object, giving a sharp image of the object against a blurred background.

Photocell
A light-sensitive cell that converts light into an electric current, used in light meters.

Projector
A machine used to display a slide, or transparency, or a movie on a screen.

Reflector
A light-colored or metallic sheet used to reflect light into shadows.

Reversal film
Film designed to produce a positive image after exposure and development, without the need to make a print from the film. Slide, or transparency, film is a reversal film and can be projected.

Still photograph
A photograph that records a scene for just a moment so that even a moving object appears still.

Stop
Another name for lens aperture.

Stopping down
Reducing the aperture size by changing the f-number from, say, f8 to f11.

TTL or "Through-The-Lens"
An in-camera metering system that measures the brightness of the light that will form the image on the film. The system usually either takes an average reading from the whole image area or a selective reading of only the central part of the image.

Viewfinder
The "sighting" system that presents the photographer with a view of the image that will be photographed.

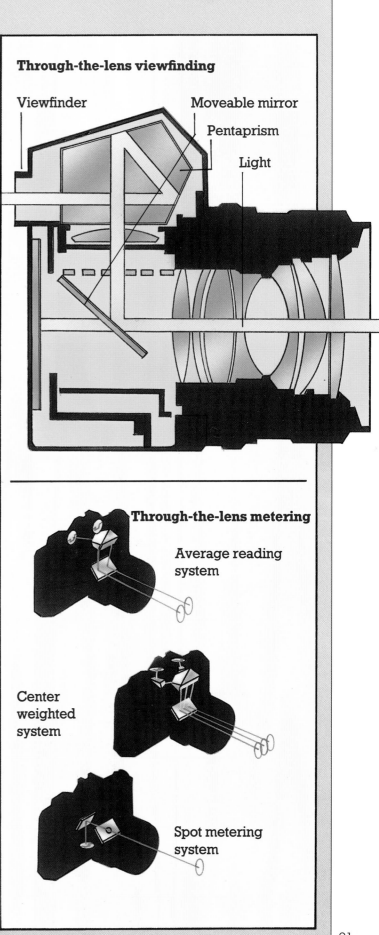

Through-the-lens viewfinding

Viewfinder

Moveable mirror

Pentaprism

Light

Through-the-lens metering

Average reading system

Center weighted system

Spot metering system

INDEX

Photographic credits
Cover and pages 6, 7 top left and right and
middle, 8, 9 both, 12 both, 13 both, 15, 19, 20,
21, 22, 23 all, 27 bottom and 29: Roger Vlitos;
page 7 bottom: The Studio Workshop; pages 9
top, 26/27 middle and 27 right: Science Photo
Library; page 10: Eye Ubiquitous; page 24 top:
The J. Allan Cash Photo Library; page 24
middle: British Film Institute; pages 24 bottom
and 26 bottom: IMAX;
pages 28 top and 28 bottom: National
Museum of Film, TV and Photography; page
28 middle: The Howarth-Loomes Collection.